The Art of Living in Joy

The Art of Living in Joy

M. Eric Donlan

BALBOA.
PRESS

A DIVISION OF HAY HOUSE

Balboa Press books may be ordered through booksellers or by contacting:

Balboa Press
A Division of Hay House
1663 Liberty Drive
Bloomington, IN 47403
www.balboapress.com
1 (877) 407-4847

Because of the dynamic nature of the Internet, any web addresses or
links contained in this book may have changed since publication and
may no longer be valid. The views expressed in this work are solely those
of the author and do not necessarily reflect the views of the publisher,
and the publisher hereby disclaims any responsibility for them.

The author of this book does not dispense medical advice or prescribe the use
of any technique as a form of treatment for physical, emotional, or medical
problems without the advice of a physician, either directly or indirectly. The
intent of the author is only to offer information of a general nature to help
you in your quest for emotional and spiritual well-being. In the event you use
any of the information in this book for yourself, which is your constitutional
right, the author and the publisher assume no responsibility for your actions.

Cover Photo Credit
François Dericq
All other photos in the book are copy written and
from the Authors private collection

Printed in the United States of America.

ISBN: 978-1-4525-1526-7 (sc)
ISBN: 978-1-4525-1528-1 (hc)
ISBN: 978-1-4525-1527-4 (e)

Library of Congress Control Number: 2014909144

Balboa Press rev. date: 06/12/2014

快乐讲堂

与心灵成长导师Eric 一起体验轻松快乐的富足人生

Eric（美国）
中文名：释宗乐

Eric是一位出色的心灵导师，更是一名成功的商人，内心深处充满着极大喜悦，经常把他的快乐和奇迹与大家分享。他师从世界知名身心灵导师Bijan（彼尚），向世人传递着和平和无条件的爱。他通过自己的身体力行，讲述着身心灵平衡之概念，引导着我们要轻松快乐的活在当下，享受身边的快乐和幸福。

Eric一直致力于Bijan（彼尚）老师"带领十亿"门心灵成长的传播，发现并验证理论把我们每个人内心深处存在的消极负面的信念系统，概括为"小我"，搞清"小我"就是制造恐惧、混乱和内疚的机器，我们每个人内心深处都存在着一个"小我"，在我们刚来到世上时，"小我"是非常渺小的，我们的能量也是最高的，灵性也都是最纯真的，高级智慧随时都会出现，我们的信念系统也是纯洁无暇的。随着慢慢的成长，我们信念系统接受到的信息越来越多，慢慢的我们就会对接收的信息产生了评判。于是，恐惧、内疚，正面与负面、正确与错误，美丽与丑恶，积极与消极等等的评判开始充斥着我们的生活，使我们每一刻都被包围着，以至于我们不能感受到宇宙带给我们的和平与爱。理论还强调我们每个人有个能量线，分为"线上"和"线下"，当我们能量在线上的时候，我们就会感到轻松快乐，感到富足，我们的"小我"也会变得很渺小。相反，就会痛苦就会贫乏，"小我"就会膨胀，很庞大。我们都想到线上去，都想过线上的生活。可是我们的"小我"是不想被变小的，他会极力的阻止我们走向线上，极力的去控制我们的线上意识。因此，我们就开始纠结，开始对未来产生恐惧，对过去产生内疚，以至于使我们的意识开始出现混乱。慢慢的，我们的能量就越来越低，以至于走到"线下"，使生活变的混乱，进而脱离现实，整日徘徊在未来和过去，不能真正的享受当下的轻松快乐和幸福！

Eric导师通过我们身边鲜活的事例，帮我们梳理着心灵上的纠结和矛盾，使我们能够放平心态，客观的对待"小我"意识的存在，引导我们的能量走向"线上"，实现轻松快乐的富足人生！他的观念就是把快乐和幸福传递给更广大的人们！实现真正意义上的和平与爱！

PROLOGUE

(Translation of excerpt from Chinese Book on page 7)
A joyful experience with mentor Eric on life and prosperity
M Eric Donlan
Chinese name: Shi, Zongle

Eric is an outstanding spiritual mentor and a successful businessman. As a teenager he was brought to NYC by his talent manager and agent and began working right away as a commercial actor and model. From there he has owned and operated many businesses such as a bagel bakery, coffee shop, antique store, café restaurant, Hallmark Store, and a Real Estate office. He holds tremendous joy within his heart and is always ready to share it with everyone. As a seeker of light, world-renowned spiritual mentors taught him. As an international speaker Eric has been spreading peace and unconditional love to the world. Through his own practice, he teaches us what it means to have balance at heart, to live in the present moment, and to embrace the joy and happiness that is always available to us when we shift our perceptions.

As a Mentor, Speaker and Life Coach, Eric has been dedicated in spreading his philosophy, which includes releasing the negative belief system lying deep within us as

our "Ego". It recognizes "Ego" as the origin of fear, chaos and guilt and we all have "Ego" within us. "Ego" starts small when we are newly born and highest on pure spiritual energy. But as we develop, our belief system receives more information upon which we place our judgment, thus the fear and guilt; positive and negative; right and wrong; beautiful and ugly; active and passive… all these judgments fill up our life and prevent us from focusing on the peace and love from the universe. "Effortless Prosperity" theory also tells our energy as "above the line" and "below the line". When our energy is "above the line", we keep our "ego" at check and tend to feel happy and content, otherwise when our ego expands and drives us into pain and misery. We all strive for "above the line" but our "ego" functions against that by tangling us with our own chaotic and negative mentality that causes our fear of the future and guilt from the past. Gradually we will lose our positive spiritual energy and step into "below the line" life where we suffer from detachment of reality, instead of living the happiness and joy of the present.

Through vivid instances, and personal stories, mentor Eric helps us to come through our spiritual struggles and conflicts, so we can watch our "ego" with open mind and objectivity. His sole purpose is to spread joy and happiness to a broader audience and guide them towards a "above the line" life where we realize our own Joyful Life, and enjoy true love and peace in every day.

CONTENTS

烈祝贺富安娜家纺 街旗舰店盛大开业 热

烈祝贺富安娜家纺上街旗舰店盛大开业

CHAPTER 1:
Life Is Joyful!

L ife is exactly what you make of it. I believe having a positive attitude is what is most important. Belief—believe in yourself, having the confidence to at least try. You do not know what you will accomplish until you try. We are all powerful, creative, unique, endowed beings. We each have the power inside to create magnificent things—just look to the past to see what other civilizations have created without any of our modern tools or electronic resources. The only thing standing in your way is yourself! Yes, I know we have all heard this before, but it is true.

Like any great skill or talent, belief in yourself takes practice. Life without limits takes a conscious effort to be open to the continuous possibilities that are presented to us. However, as we redefine our belief system and learn to let go of the baggage holding us back—our anger, resentment, grievances, and fear—our path will open up effortlessly. Each day becomes easier to connect to the people and opportunities around us. Happiness comes from inside; it's a natural state of being that allows you to handle whatever life brings your way. When you view all events as just experiences and leave your judgment out of it, you are open to a whole new spectrum of ways to view and also to handle these things. I am able to say this only by looking at my own life and seeing what I have been able to achieve and experience while maintaining my joyful spirit.

My childhood and early years were less than normal. I did not grow up in the typical American happy family— does it really exist anywhere? I did not have a father; he died a month before I was born. My mother and I lived with my grandmother, great-grandmother, and uncle. We did live in a very nice New England town named Melrose. On Main Street, up many stairs, sat our typical Victorian house with a wraparound porch and two staircases inside. I enjoyed running up one set and down the other; this proved useful when I was being chased to try to avoid punishment from some mischief I was up to. I remember being a happy child, but the arguing of my mother and grandmother often shattered this peace. They could really go at it, and at times they got physical by throwing toasters and other small appliances at each other. We even had a cabinet in the basement with broken items. I don't know why they saved them. I think it was part of their issue of never letting anything go—especially the things inside: anger, grudges, and resentment. These are the things that hold so many people back from having the lives that they desire.

I remember feeling sad at these times of arguing. I would go into my own creative world to escape. My grandmother had all the old Ed Sullivan records of famous musicals and singers, and I would play them up in my room and act out the story or sing along. I fantasized about performing and being part of something special. I think this was when I realized that I did not want to be involved in the negative energy of anger. I knew deep inside that I desired peace, contentment, and love. However, at the time all I felt was loneliness and confusion because of the way my family interacted.

Being an only child with a working parent did have its advantages. My mother worked hard but always provided very well for me. Some would say I was a little spoiled, but what parent doesn't want a better life for their kid than they had? I didn't have a lot of rules or guidance. I realized later on in life that this was more because of her lack of parenting skill and not from a lack of care. She did not learn much from her mother about being a mother; my mother's was not a happy childhood.

Ann, my mother, was the oldest of five children with a

very abusive father and an uncommunicative mother. I knew from the beginning that my mother never wanted a child; I was somewhat of a mistake, created from a bad situation. She did the best she could with the resources she had—Ann was responsible in everything to a fault. Eventually I came to realize that even though she didn't want to "bring another life into this crowded world," she was glad that it was me. I was well provided for and given many opportunities that other children never had. I was usually treated as a peer rather than a child, which was good and bad. My time was my own, and I became independent at a very young age because I scared off all the sitters. Everyone in the house worked, so I was left to my own devices.

I was included in more conversations and arguments than I should have been for my young age. My grandmother was extremely outspoken and always expressed her opinion, as twisted and bigoted as it was. I remember trying to digest at an early age my grandmother saying that my mother wanted to give me up for adoption and she would not let her do that because I would have ended up in a black family. I still cannot understand to this day her warped view on many things.

These experiences somehow forged into me a very strong spirit and sense of self. I did not feel I could rely on those around me to provide me with love or happiness, so I had to go within and find my own strength. Eventually I went out into the world to experience life and learn about myself. On a deep level I knew that if I were to find happiness, it would have to come from me.

I learned to not let these elements of my childhood get to me. I used them for my advantage. At an early age of eight, I began traveling alone by air to visit relatives. I was very lucky to have family that lived in California and New York. My one aunt, my mother's sister; my cousin, her daughter; and my great aunt, who was a Salvation Army minister, lived on Long Island. My great aunt ran a big church and summer Bible school with many wonderful caring people. I believe this place was the beginning of my blessings. My experiences there gave me great balance in my life, learning about God and religion and some life truths that would later become the foundation for my spiritual awareness.

I remember flying on Eastern Airlines from Boston to New York City and getting a shiny pair of pilot wings—they were real metal back then, not plastic like today. I was very outgoing and talked to everyone. I enjoyed the attention a minor got back then when traveling alone. It was exciting, and I learned quickly that there was a great big world out there, waiting to be explored.

Every school vacation I was on a plane to Long Island or California, where my other great aunts and uncles lived.

They had a more traditional family with a mom and dad, family dinners, fun outings to amusement parks, ball games, car pools, and such. I was able to see and feel what it was like to be part of a traditional family, and I became aware of things I wanted to create in my life in the future. I never focused on what I didn't have; I thought about what I would have to do to create those things for myself. I saw possibilities in life—if someone else could do it or have it, so could I. The hard part at the time was figuring out how!

My mother always supported me, at least financially, in any activity I was interested in pursuing. In grade school it was a brand-new slide trombone. Why? I have no idea. I think it was big and looked cool, and I remembered the song "Seventy-Six Trombones" from the *Music Man*, one of the musicals I listened to as a child. Then it was drama class at Discovery Workshop, a neat community theater group run by one of my friend's parents. I loved going there and learned to express myself better. I became even more comfortable performing in front of people.

I know I was lucky to travel. The many summers spent with my aunt Major Dorothy Saunders, were wonderful years and I remember them very fondly. Every Sunday was church, and then during the week was day camp for kids when school was out, and for 2 weeks in August we were inspired by a visiting evangelist, Miss Ruth, who taught the vacation bible school. I believe these years were very inspirational and integral in forming my good set of basic values, Love, compassion, joy, kindness, just to name a few. The teachers and mentors I met through my Aunt also inspired me spiritually. They made the many bible stories in Sunday school come alive with felt boards, characters or puppets. Even as a child I would sit in during my Aunts bible studies, usually just playing, but I guess I must have been listening on a deeper level. Being there I definitely felt loved. As a cute kid with a lot of energy, I also got a lot of attention from the senior members of the congregation. They always willing to give a good hug or a quarter to buy an ice cream! I think this was also the beginning of my entrepreneurial spirit. I remember one summer when my cousin Melanie and I made perfume from the many flowers and trees that were on the four-acre church property and we sold small bottles of it to the senior citizens.

As a young teen, I went into Boston to explore and go about the city in search of adventure. My favorite place to go was the Ritz-Carlton Hotel near the Boston Common. I don't remember what attracted me to that place, but I liked the style, the elegance, and the spa. A manicure became my favorite Saturday activity. Around the corner on Newberry Street, I would go to a fashionable hair salon to get a haircut. I liked to take care of myself, and I believed I was worth it.

This knowing came from within me—I knew that I was special. I often felt I didn't belong where I was, because I had always been very different from my family. My grandmother always said that they had no idea where my "Little Lord Fauntleroy" tastes came from.

On one of my Saturday excursions into the city, I wandered past a sign for a modeling agency and decided to go into the office. I wanted to be a model. Deep inside I knew I could create anything I really wanted to, and I did. I was placed into a talent and fashion show in Boston, which I won. I went to New York City to compete in the finals. The show in New York City was an exciting experience; I began to really feel like I was living my dream. I was signed by a manager and an agent and began working right away. I booked my first commercial that I auditioned for.

At the age of seventeen, I moved to New York City to pursue my acting career. I finished high school in a special program called City-As-School, which was exciting because I got to attend some classes at New York University as well as the New School for Social Research. I had a flexible schedule that allowed me to do my acting work, take special performing classes, and finish my senior year of high school while earning college credit. It was very cool, and I was on a high! I was featured in many national television commercials, radio ads, and was a print model for many national stores.

I was also booked as a day player on a few soap operas, and movies. Live theatre was my favorite. My most amazing memory was the summer I was part of the "Othello" cast starring Avery Brooks and Andre Braugher. Even then I was living my dream, but not really aware of how I was creating it.

I was very proud when I graduated, and my family came to my school in New York City to attend the ceremony. I gave a speech at graduation, which even today amazes me because my philosophy was so evident back then. This speech was written almost thirty years ago, and I can see how connected I was, but I didn't really understand it or have much clarity. Looking back, I see how and where my philosophy on life started. Everything is connected, and I see so many miracles in my life.

HIGH SCHOOL GRADUATION SPEECH, 1984
Choices
by M. Eric Donlan

Life is a series of choices. That which we are is that which we have chosen to be. That which we will become is that which we choose to become! We are all in control of our lives and destiny.

We do choose our own course. Even though some people decide to adhere to others' expectations of what they should become in life, that in itself is still a choice. Those with strong character insist on making all their own choices despite the opinions of others. Life choices are difficult. It is hard to determine the right course to take at times. I have learned to trust my instincts. The right decision usually comes in time.

No matter what the outcome, I still feel good about the choice—even if it turns out to be a mistake! Mistakes are only opportunities to learn from. Choice and action always outweigh indecision and apprehension. Try not to let those things hold you back. In every situation there is always something new to learn. Approach each experience as if it were the first time you beheld it. Possibilities abound when you look for them. Examine each new step in life with past experience and current expectation to determine which choice to make. Nothing in itself is ever dull or exciting— it is only how we personally perceive it. If we see things positively, we will create positive results.

Nothing can affect us that we won't let affect us. We make life what it is—and what it isn't. The quicker we face reality and the sooner we begin to control the direction of our lives, the better they will become. Attract positive, get positive! Live in the present; experience each day one at a time. Savor each and every moment. I'm not saying we shouldn't plan ahead, but work at achieving smaller goals that ascend to your peak. Slow and steady does win the race. Anxiety kills the best of deals. Everyone wants to succeed, but it usually takes time. Patience, give me patience—but hurry up already! Everyone has the ability to become successful; it is your choice what to do with your gifts. Remember, the only person who stands in our way is ourselves.

So *get out of your own way*—enjoy life and all that it can bestow. Take in as much as possible, but keep humble. Live in gratitude. Appreciate the small gifts. No matter how much you know, there is always more to be learned. Respect yourself, and others will too! Regardless of what we create in life, *all* of us possess the necessary capabilities to make our own choices and determine our own destiny. Aside from being the ones that make the choices, we also determine the various possibilities from which to pick. Life—it is *my choice!*

CHAPTER 2:
Attitude and Attraction

I am excited to share my thoughts with you. Through my stories and sharing some of my life experiences, my goal is to assist you in creating new ways of looking at challenging situations. I want to inspire you to see things through a new perspective. If you change your perception, you can change your whole life!

The law of attraction is fueled by your attitude. The outcome of an event is largely predicated upon the state of mind with which you enter the event. If you go in with a positive attitude, you will create positive results. What you focus on, you create. Good or bad, what you resist, persists. What you insist, you manifest! Your attitude creates *magnitude*! Happiness begins inside. Think about it: if you meet someone on the street and smile, usually you will get a smile in return. If you come from a place of peace and kindness, you will spark that same flame in another person. Positive energy begets positive emotion, but it has to begin somewhere. Use your initiative and take the first step. Be the first one to give out positive energy. Be conscious of all you have to be thankful for; we each have so many small blessings we take for granted. What you send out to the universe, you get back in abundance.

There is a difference between trying and doing. Have you ever tried to pick up a pencil? You can't! You either pick it up or you don't. An attitude of trying to do something just gives you an out or an excuse if you fail. "Well, I tried!" It just won't work. An attitude of success with total commitment, backed by 100 percent action, will bring you to your goal. Have faith that with perseverance you *can* create the blessings and accomplishments you want in your life. Be the answer that you want to see in your life and in the world.

Your attitude really sets the course your day will take. In the morning I like to mentally focus on what I have to be thankful for and what I want to accomplish with my day. I stretch and do my yoga and connect with the energy of the day. I want to center myself and open up to receiving guidance. My ultimate goal is always to have peace and joy in my life. I know that I am created whole and complete. We all have the same potential—the question is how are we going to direct and use our daily energies? Sometimes I make a to-do list. Sometimes I just plan things out in my mind. Find what works best for you—a road map for the day!

By making a list you can keep focused and check things off as you do them. You will find that when you focus and put things out into the universe, the universe will assist you in accomplishing what you need to do. Your days will become effortless. Actively participate in your life and enjoy the journey. Right here, right now—look at what you have. Notice your blessings. Always come from appreciation and gratitude. All of your strength and opportunity will come from this connection. Every event in our lives is a blessing. We may not know the meaning at the moment, but if we trust, the bigger picture will be revealed in perfect time. Every event is for our higher good.

Yesterday, today, and tomorrow—what day do you live in? Do events bring you frustration, anger, and resentment or joy, happiness, and delight? We are not victims. On some level we have asked for the situation we are encountering. We are always creating our reality. It's just a question of whether you are creating it consciously or unconsciously.

Where we focus our attention is what we are manifesting in our lives. You just have to look around and see what is going on in your life to see where your attention has been focused. If you do not like what you see, change your focus. Be willing to let go, and allow the way for a new choice.

You do not have to keep repeating the same disappointing experiences again and again.

Don't be bound by your perceptions. Do you really know the meaning of what you see? You are only interpreting it based on your current situation. When you shift your perception, you may see things totally differently and with a new perspective. By looking at the bigger picture, you may become aware of a solution or a resolution to whatever experience you are having at the present moment. By changing your mind about how you feel about something, you clear the way for the energy to flow and guide you to a new place and a new experience.

The universe accommodates your expectations. It is very important to set up your inner expectations in a positive manner in order to be sure you achieve the goal you wish to attain. As I have said before, your thoughts create your reality. It is very important to prepare your mind before you begin to work on a project. Do the emotional work first, from the inside out. Your thoughts, your belief systems, should be in alignment with your actions and goals. How do you feel about where you are wanting to go or wanting to do? Create a clear, deep knowing that you are confident, capable, and self-assured. When you do this, you will attract what you want to manifest into your life. There will be no maybes! You will consciously create and attract with the certainty that you are a powerful creator, as you were born to be. This is our inheritance, every one of us.

I had a speaking event in Beijing and I needed to be there by 11:00 a.m. Monday morning. My assistant had booked me on a 10:00 p.m. Sunday night flight from Zhengzhou to Beijing. I was coming from another event in Kaifeng, and that was the only flight I could make. My schedule is always pretty busy and each day is planned out, but the weather doesn't always cooperate. I arrived at my home in Zhengzhou about 7:00 p.m., quickly changed clothes, and repacked for Beijing. The car picked me up at 8:00 p.m. and drove me to the airport. I got to the airport only to find that the flight was canceled—not delayed, just canceled! I found the Air China desk, but there was no Air China staff anywhere. There were other airline staff, but no one from Air China could be found.

By now there were lots of other angry passengers gathering around the same desk, all talking with each other in Chinese. What I could pick up from my limited Chinese was "Where are the workers?" and "Why are there no flights?" There was a nice China Southern Airline worker there who was trying to help us; she was phoning Air China, looking for a representative. But there was no one! She could not find any Air China workers who could assist us. All she could tell us was that the weather in Beijing was very bad and all the flights were canceled for the night.

Knowing that their flight was canceled, I could not believe that Air China did not have a representative there to help the customers. I thought that this was very bad business. But to the credit to the China Southern worker, she was very helpful and at least tried to help. It wasn't her problem, but she did make an effort. Most people didn't do this; most people just wanted to complain and be angry. They were venting about the problem and how badly they were affected by it. They wanted to wallow in playing the role of the victim.

What do you do when confronted with a problem? Do

you just complain? Do you play the victim, or do you take action? Most people want to be part of the problem. I suggest looking at things differently and creating a solution. It is an opportunity to change your perception and see things differently. Allowing is very important in this process. Some events I cannot change or control, but I can decide how I will respond to them. I shift my focus to "What can I do in this situation? How can I turn things around?"

I always look for the opportunity, the other perspective. *This is a chance to have a new experience, an adventure*, I thought to myself. I had to be in Beijing by 10:00 a.m. the next morning to do a seminar. The first thing that came into my mind was the possibility of a train; I had never taken a train to Beijing. I called out in the crowd and said, "Anyone going to the train station? Does anyone know English? Anyone understand me?" Two people actually said yes. One woman, who spoke very good English, was on her cell phone with a friend, booking her on a train the next day. She said, "Oh, I can get you a ticket with me tomorrow." To which I replied, "Thank you, but I need to be in Beijing by tomorrow." Then a young gentleman, who spoke only broken English, said he was just on the phone and got the last seat on the train to Beijing. I asked him if he could call the booking office and see if there was anything else available. The young man called but got the same response: all the tickets for that night were sold out.

Well, I knew the universe loved me and I had to get to where I was going. I know when I need to trust and just keep moving forward. I asked the young man if I could travel with him to the train station. I would check again at the window.

We arrived at the chaos that is a Chinese train station and pushed our way to the ticket window—no one lines up in China! The young man asked the clerk about tickets. I understand that she was saying no. I asked her to keep looking. Suddenly she found something on a train one hour before the other one. The journey would be longer than the fast four-hour trip, but it would get me into Beijing by 8:00 a.m. Perfect!

The train was a sleeper compartment, and I actually got eight hours sleep, a longer sleep than I would have gotten if I had flown and gone to the hotel. In addition, this timing allowed for the young man to put me on the train, which was great; otherwise, it would have been very confusing. All the signs were in Chinese! The train was also much cheaper than the airplane, only RMB 165 compared to RMB 800. I saved RMB 600 on the transportation, and I saved RMB 400 on the hotel. I saved over RMB 1000 and had a better night's sleep just by trusting and following my instincts.

I share this story with you because I know we are all faced with similar situations. Trust that if you pause for a moment and look for the solution, rather than complain, your higher self will lead you to the path that is best for you. Most people go into their head and voice their opinions, looking for sympathy. Playing a victim seems so much easier. But please realize you give all your power away when you do that. Understand that on some level you created the situation; your decisions led to it. You are now in control. Once we are aware of that, we can do something about it. We are the creators of our reality. When we embrace this truth, we are then empowered to make change. Your attitude determines the outcome. Right here, right now, take control, take a new path, and make a new choice. Take the power back and create in your life what you really desire. Don't create by default. Consciously create!

Having a positive attitude is key. We are all in this together. Originally we all come into this world open. As children we are eager, happy. We come into this world with love and enthusiasm. Everything seems interesting and an exciting opportunity to discover. When I was a young child, I could make anything a toy. Everything had possibilities. A cardboard box became a spaceship; a pile of leaves could be formed into a racecar; odds and ends could create a shop or market. I loved to be creative and use my imagination. But as we grow, we hear adults say how hard life is and how you can't live in a land of make-believe. We hear, "Don't do that! That's dangerous! That is not good for you! You are not able to do that; you could get hurt!" We begin to start forming these negative belief systems.

We begin to think of ourselves as limited. The reality is that we are unlimited. Our minds seem to fill with thoughts of what we are not, rather than the possibility we possess.

My goal is for us all to know that we are incredibly wonderful people. We are all powerful creators blessed with different gifts that make each of us special in our own way. If we step back, there is always something in our life we can be thankful for. These are simple truths that will empower us and carry us through once we are aware of them. We can get all the things we want out of life; it just takes practice. Like any athlete wanting to be the best he or she can be, you train your mind to be aware and consciously create. It takes work. It takes practice. The more you pay attention to your thought process and where you focus your attention, the easier it will become. You will automatically begin to see the opportunities again. Inspiration will flow and life will become easier and effortless. Fun and excitement will return, along with your confidence and security.

Think about what is really holding you back: thoughts of "I can't" or "I'm not good enough, not smart enough, not good looking enough." These are all lies your mind makes up for reasons not to try. They are all just limiting excuses. Get out of your head and into your heart. It's not about finding a formula, it's about getting connected to who you really are and the potential you possess. Believe in all the things that you want to become because they are already inside you. It is that belief and connection that will bring them into reality. There is an old saying that tells us to "dress for the job you want, not for the job you have." The same can be said about your life. Truly accept and believe you are worthy and capable of becoming all that you desire, and you will surely create it. If you can conceive it and believe it, you will achieve it!

Wake up to your own power, because it is there! When you reach out and do, you can create miracles. Life is about doing and experiencing. You will never get wet if you do not go into the water.

CHAPTER 3:
Reality and Truth

W hat is truth? What is reality? What is illusion? Mass consciousness wants to perpetuate problems and focus on what is wrong. We need to be solution-focused. Always be looking for the most positive thought we can have in any given situation. Reality is just what people believe in at any one time. This is what the mass consciousness believes. But that reality changes over time. For example, at one point in time the wise people on this planet believed it to be flat and that it was the center of the universe. People believed beyond any doubt that if you sailed too far, you would fall off the edge of the earth. The truth is that the earth is round and rotates around the sun.

Truth does not change, but it is constantly expanding. Illusion occurs in your mind. Often it is what you quickly perceive in a moment, but it is not really what is going on. We all have unconscious belief systems, which we have created though our life experiences. Scientists have found that most people react 95 percent of the time from the unconscious mind based on the illusion they think they see. When we are aware and in the moment, we are open to see the reality or, better yet, the truth in any experience. Only then can we make a conscious choice, which will most probably have a positive outcome.

Love, joy, hope, happiness, and success—they are the "right here, right now." They are where you find your strength and opportunity. What I see most people living in is an illusion that they create in the mind through fear. We carry so much anger, fear, guilt, and resentment that we are weighed down. Unhappiness seems to be the theme of many people. Resistance is where the mind goes when confronted by a difficult situation. Saying "I can't" just gives people an excuse to fail. Does this get you anywhere? No! I suggest changing your question to "What can I do?"

Maybe you don't understand the whole solution at the moment, but thinking in a positive direction will allow you to move in the right direction. Think about what you have to do today to get one step closer to where you want to be tomorrow. Be in the present moment. The simple formula to deal with any situation is to connect, discover, and respond.

The magic is in the connection. People really don't

connect much anymore. We go around with our earphones in, listening to music, or we have our cell phones glued to our ear, chatting away and not noticing all the wonderful things around us. I see people sitting at the same table, texting each other and not really communicating. Parents aren't interested in their children. Children do not care about their parents. Employers are only concerned with the production of the workers and the metrics. They have lost touch with who they are and why they are doing what they are doing. The "why" and "who" are important. The connection is important.

Every choice that you make has a result. Every action has a reaction. Everyone has one past, one present, and many futures. The present is the truth. That is the reality. When you see that moment clearly, then you can make a choice to give you a positive result. Your past does not dictate your future unless you do not use your power of the present.

If you think, *Well, I can't do this because that will happen,* or relate the moment to a limiting past experience, you limit yourself. You give your power away and disconnect yourself from the universal force of energy that can guide you. When fear comes up, you must dismiss it and think, *What can I do?* One past, one present, and many future possibilities—this is based on your conscious choice in the moment. Many people give away this power by just reacting in the moment and *not* choosing what direction to go.

Some say it's just my Karma. The truth is that Karma does not really exist in the realm of truth. Karma exists in reality only because people believe it. Karma only happens if you allow it into your experience. As I have said, you always create what you think about and believe. Karma is just another belief system if you allow it into your experience and surrender your power to it. Karma is when you don't take your power of choice and you disconnect from your source energy and then create unconsciously or by default. You are manifesting unconsciously. Karma is just giving your power away. It does not really exist at the source level. It is a belief the mind has made up to justify why you can't take action and change your situation. What is really going on is the law of cause and effect. You always create and attract what you believe and think about. Make a conscious choice today to have the result you want tomorrow. We all have the power to create our future just the way we want it to be.

Life is our choice. That which we choose is that which we are going to create. Creation begins in the mind, which ignites desire, creating wanting, which paves the way and brings about manifestation through inspired action. When you are connected to the source energy, which is available to us all at every moment, everything seems to come together and align to your desires. But if you have a negative belief system around you and believe this is just the way it is, you create a negative result. You are always going to create what you think about. My goal is to put the power back in your hands, where it has really been all the time. I am only here to remind you of your inheritance and that there is never a time you are disconnected from your source. It is always there, just waiting patiently for you to remember, to realize it in the present moment. The simple truth that I want to explain to you is that at every moment we have the choice to make something good happen by consciously choosing; or we can make something bad happen by giving our power away. Not making a choice or going along the way of the mass consciousness will lead to an undesired result or something that will give you emotional discomfort.

Most of the mass consciousness lives in virtual reality—this place that is not truth; the place of just reacting to the stimulus in your own universe; the world of fear, anxiety, angst, scarcity; a place where people play the victim, the pity role; the "why me" place. That is the world most people live in. People in this place want to pull you down with them; it makes them feel better to think that there are others just like them, which justifies in their mind why they are not able to take action and change their situation. Do you know someone who goes to you and dumps all their "stuff" on you when something bad happens to them? They think you should feel sorry for them. People want to give you stories, trying to justify why they are in the situation they are in. But the stories are not real; it's just them wanting to bring you down, lower your energy. If you have experienced this situation, don't you just feel drained after? All it does is perpetuate fear and anxiety. Yes, the boogeyman does exist—you must beware and be afraid!

But no situation is solved through fear. Focusing on the problem just perpetuates the problem. How can you be a vibrational match to the solution of your situation when all you do is hold your energy in the lower place by rehashing it again and again?

My goal is for you to recognize that moment when you have a choice. Do you want to go this way and maybe pull others down, or do you want to make a different choice? This is an awareness that will serve you in all areas of your life. Everything is connected to the present moment and the choices you make in it! I wish for everyone to have a happy life, a balanced life.

I want to wake you up to the simple truth that we have a choice in every moment. Do you want to be part of the problem or part of the solution?

When you want to get from here to there, don't come from your head and wonder how you are going to do it. How can I get way over there? If I come from my head and from mass consciousness, I begin to ponder all the mechanics involved. For example, I have to raise my left leg, I have to bend my knee, and I have to shift my weight to the other side. I have to bring my back leg up, then shift it forward, and bring it down—it's a lot of work. It sounds like there is great effort involved. That is attacking the problem from the mind; it's complicating the situation. That's focusing on the problem. What I am saying is that if you want to get from here to there, just do it! Go to the "right here, right now" moment. Trust in the inspired action that will come when you put your desire out there. The universal energy like a current of water will carry you to your goal. Doors will open, and cooperative components will come together to assist. You will find the action or work that you are doing along the way is joyful and fun. And best of all, it is very satisfying. Getting to your goal can be fun and easy!

CHAPTER 4:
Connect, Discover, Respond!

I only live in the now, this present moment. Most people live in the past and future, but these are not reality. It is a time made up in the mind, a place where fear and angst live. They are places that foster worry or regret. Whenever I am in the past or future, I am not—ego is.

Most discussion is brought about by ego, being not in the moment, artificial reality. Most of the meaning we try to put on things is only our misperception of that moment, trying to figure things out rather than just being very present in the moment and letting the information or the experience enter us. This is how we become really aware, being present in the moment and really taking in whatever is going on.

When you get up each day, let go of what happened yesterday. Don't let it define your present state. Release what was, and be open to a new experience. Be open to seeing something differently than you did the day before. This is how I get through difficult situations: keeping my mind fresh and open to new possibilities, and being able to shift my perceptions. Maybe I will notice a new solution I was not aware of before.

Think of it like this: When a deer wakes up each day in the forest, do you think she begins the day rehashing what happened yesterday or complaining about her current situation? "Oh, wow! I am glad I'm still alive. I had a bad scare with the hunters. I was almost shot. Oh my gosh! If I am not careful, the same thing will happen today. What will I do? Who will take care of my fawn if something happens to me?" No! All of this is a made-up story. This is what stresses and ages us. This drains us of our energy and clouds our mind.

When a deer awakes, it looks around. It sees what is around. It realizes it is hungry and thirsty. These are the only things that are important. They are in the moment. The deer knows which direction to take because it actually looks. It sees if the way is safe, clear, and quiet, and it goes that direction. A deer reacts instinctually. If a wolf jumps out at it, it runs. It does not clutter its mind by trying to figure out why the wolf is coming at it. The deer does not try to analyze the situation. Rather, it just reacts. Many people have forgotten this and go blindly on routine. They do the same thing day after day and are somewhat unaware of what is really around them. Many people are on automatic. When you are in this state, you cannot make a clear decision or react quickly in a given situation. You need to be in the present—right here, right now. That is the key. This is where your power comes from. Your awareness of the situation is vastly improved. You are able to really see what is going on and evaluate your options.

Belief systems and reality—what is real and what is illusion?

What you bring to thought is a belief system, your preconceived notions of things. What you think you are seeing at the moment is usually *not* what you are really seeing at the moment.

What I really know is now, this moment. This is what is real. This is the place where change can happen. This is the place and time for a new choice. When we are aware, we have the opportunity to make a conscious, clear choice. When you are aware and in the moment, you have the tool to help you to facilitate your daily quest for happiness.

Life works and is effortless when things flow. If we take each present moment and make the right choice to bring us closer to our goal, we will get the results we are looking for. This is the same in all aspects of our life. Our relationships,

our work, our health, and our financial well-being are what
primarily concern all of us. But how do we get in the flow
and balance all this? Just like the answer of the saying "How
do you get to Carnegie Hall?" you get there through practice,
practice, practice. Consciously be aware of when you are in
the moment and when you are not. It is best to do this with
no judgment, no right or wrong. Just notice where you are.
It will get easier with time and the more you are aware. This
is a simple tool I use to always be present and aware in each
moment. I think connect, discover, and respond.

What is connecting? It is the art of knowing. What is
going on in the present moment? What is the truth in front of
me? It is not what am I interpreting based on past experience,
but what is really happening. I must let go of any past emotion
that comes up and consider what I am experiencing in the
moment. Rather than just reacting, I want to think about
my options. I should pause for a moment and notice how I
am feeling in an experience. Just look inside and see what
emotion is coming up. Feel it, sense it, and really connect
to the energy of the situation. What or who do we need to
connect with? Do we know what is expected of us in each
moment? What is the role we must take on to accomplish
the task at hand? We need to communicate and listen to the
people and things around us to answer these questions and
achieve our goal. There are always opportunities available

when we are present and aware that will help us to position ourselves to get the best results.

Some good connecting exercises begin with visually noticing the things and people around us. Then add in the sounds and voices and really take them in, Observe, process, and think about what you are seeing and hearing. Use all your senses to gather as much information as possible. The sights, sounds, smells, and tastes are the details that make up the moment. This is where the juice is—the nectar! Once we are truly present and connected, we can than discover what is going on inside ourselves, and also what is going on around us.

That is the next step—discover. Once you have observed and taken in the moment, discover what is there. Using the information you have just gathered, think about what is genuinely relevant. Turn things over and look at things more closely. Ask discovery questions: What is expected of me? What do I want to happen? What are the possible outcomes? What is my goal? What steps should I take to achieve my goal? Consider the possibilities. Take a few moments to ponder and open your mind to the greater wisdom that is available to us all. What am I emotionally feeling inside about the person or situation in front of me? What is the best result that will make me feel good and bring me peace and joy? These are the things to discover in any situation that will allow you to be aware of the truth in the moment and feel your inspired response.

Do whatever you have to do to get a clear understanding of the moment at hand. Communication is also a great tool used to discover. But even more important than talking is listening! Once the questions are asked, we must always actively listen. That is the key to good communication. Listening and understanding are fundamental. If I were to be granted three wishes, the first would be to speak and understand all the languages in the world. I believe all issues can be solved with clear, direct communication. Most problems arise out of fear and misunderstanding. We are all here in the world to help each other; there really is enough good to go around for all of us. These are the basics of teamwork and how major feats are accomplished more easily. Take some responsibility. Be accountable. Be the change you want to see in the world. So many people talk about what is wrong or broken in life, but no one takes action.

While working in the many different businesses I have owned, the worst response that I heard much too often was "Well, that's not my job." I have news for you! Everything is your responsibility. We are all powerful creators, and our energy can have a huge effect in the world when we understand this and come into alignment with it.

Finally, respond. By using everything that you have gathered, you must respond to the situation at hand and take action based on your inspiration. Take action, but keep it fun and enjoyable. If you are in alignment with the moment and your goal, the action or work will seem effortless and enjoyable. Make good choices and respond with passion. What you think about in your mind is what is going to manifest in your life.

Energy is always flowing, and things will always work out when you allow yourself to be moved by the current and act in the situation. Believe in yourself and take the path that brings you the best feeling. There is a great difference between working and trying to take action against a problem and taking inspired action toward the solution. We can't solve a problem by focusing on it; we must focus on the solution. Always reach for the best thought or best emotion you can in any situation. Let that lead you to your course of action—inspired response! My goal is to be able to make a clear, positive choice, the best choice, *right here, right now.* That will keep me feeling happy and joyful. This is the active choice that flows through me by being connected to my source energy.

Use this simple formula in any situation: connect, discover, respond. Connect with life around you. By openly observing, listening, and being aware of the situation going on in your experience, you will be connected to whatever action the moment may require. This allows you to be objective, without attachment or judgment. Allow yourself to be completely open to see the truth in any circumstance. Discover the truth of the moment.

Take one day at a time, one moment at a time. Where are you going to focus your energy? Where are you going to focus your attention? Release your worry and fear. When you think and focus on these elements, it just perpetuates the problem. It's a vicious circle. Break this cycle and practice being hopeful and optimistic. Always direct your thoughts to successful, positive things. Feeling capable, loved, and connected are the keys to fully participating in life. Be determined to consciously create a happy and joyful life.

We are consistently expanding, creating new things, and opening our minds to new thought. We are creating each new day one at a time. Maintain a good attitude, live with passion, and keep the excitement of life alive. There is always a way to include joy in everything you are doing.

CHAPTER 5:
Right Here, Right Now

The law of attraction begins with *awareness*! Notice what is going on around you. Notice what you are feeling. Be conscious of your environment. Be aware of your actions and others' reactions. Take responsibility for the *now*. Live every day in the moment. To take advantage of an opportunity, you need to see it coming. Know your gifts and skills, and be ready to use them. Be aware of the present. Most people live in the past or the future, either regretting what has happened to them or worrying what would or could happen in the future. What has happened in the past is the past! Be defined by the choices you make today, not the ones you made yesterday. Get over it, move on, and move forward. If you want to change your future, you need to take action *today*. Live in the present and utilize the power of now. If I want it to be, it's up to me. Right here, right now, I am my power—I am it.

Find your passion in life; find your excitement, whatever it takes to keep your energy up. We live in a vibrational universe. In order to get where you are going, you need to feel like you are there and be open to seeing the evidence along the way. If you don't see something in your immediate universe to bring your energy up, then shift your attention to something that will give you comfort in the moment or ease the stress you are feeling. Sometimes it takes baby steps when we are in the middle of a problem, but keep going in the direction of up, not down or in the midst, which will only make matters continue. Life is a circle, and we are all part of that circle.

Think about the passion that children have. It does not matter what the situation is; they can always draw on their infinite imagination and excitement. Each situation is just an experience. If you can stop judging and reacting from fear and just take a moment to pause and look at things objectively, you can harness your power and connections. You can clearly choose what path, what course of action is in your highest good. Look inside, listen to your heart, your inner guidance, and you can get through any experience positively. If you believe in yourself and you believe that you are capable and confident, you will be. The answer or the solution will appear when you are in touch with your higher self. The best of times are now. In each moment find your passion, your truth, and your joy. All your power comes from the now—right here, right now!

I notice that most people are careful and aware about their money. How they earn it, how they save it, and how they spend it. Why do they not think the same about their time? I find my time is my most precious commodity. When a day is gone, when an hour is gone, it is no more. You cannot get it back no matter how hard you try. I notice many people waste their time. They are careful with money but not with time. I want to remind you how precious your time really is. I say, "I love to live, and I live to love!" What that means is for every moment of every day, every experience I have, my goal is to live fully and with joy.

That is being in the present moment. If you are really living in the present, you will get the outcome that you genuinely desire. The answers will appear, especially if we share with each other and come from love. Have love be our motive—not what can I get but what can I give. How can I contribute and fully experience this moment? The more love that I give, the more I feel I get back. Wherever I go, I always connect with people and engender happiness and joy from them. Whether it's a smile or a hug, giving genuine love will always manifest love in return. We all desire love; we are all the same inside. We want to feel love, share love, and be accepted for who we are. We want to be happy; it is our natural state of being. The little child inside of us wants to be happy, wants to love, wants to experience and be joyful. Break through those limiting beliefs and the judgment that hold us back from claiming all that is ours. Joy will bring you the answer; joy will bring you a solution that works. I cannot explain why or how it works, but if you focus on having peace and joy in your life—and make that your first goal—everything else will fall into place. This is a universal law. When you come from joy and happiness and connect with the energy that flows through everything, life works. We fulfill what we are here to do.

So many people say they want this to work or that to work. They are discontent with the way of the world: war, famine, and natural disasters. They complain about their home life, children, family, etc. The state of their city or country bothers them. Many talk about world peace. I ask you, what are you doing on a daily basis to create a better future? What part are you playing? Are you part of the problem or part of the solution?

Nothing changes by focusing or complaining about "what is." That only perpetuates it. Bring your energy to the solution; think about what you can do to make things better. Time is precious. The change we want to see in the world must always begin with each of us. If you make the choices in each moment of every day that will bring you a beneficial outcome in every situation you are presented with, that will change not only your life but also the lives of the people you touch. When you come from joy, when your goal is happiness each day, people will notice the difference in you and be attracted to it. Tomorrow shouldn't be the focus; today is what is here. The choices today, each day, create your tomorrow. Today is what is important.

What you think about, where you focus your attention is what you will manifest in your life. We are all amazing creators, just most people create unconsciously or by default. My goal is for us all to be aware of what we are creating moment by moment. Be a victorious creator, not a victim of your creations! If you are not getting the results in life that you want, honestly look at yourself and say, "What am I doing that is giving me these results?" or "What haven't I been willing to do to get what I want in life?" We create the good as well as the bad; it's only when we take responsibility for our life that we can regain the control and direct it in the direction we truly desire. It all comes back to the present moment. Every action always has a reaction. Be aware of the action you are taking.

The secret to life is to live each day fully, passionately, knowing that you are loved and supported by the source that connects us all. Whatever presents itself in each moment, just experience it. Allow it. Just say yes. Notice how you are feeling inside, and listen for your inner voice to guide you to inspired action. Events are not good or bad, they just are. They are all just experiences. It's your thoughts and judgments that bring up emotion and confusion. Use "right here, right now" to give you clarity. Live each day in the present. We have the power of choice. We can choose where we want to focus our mind. We are all incredibly powerful creators; we just need to create consciously. What do I really want to happen in this moment? What is the outcome that I truly desire for my highest good? Do you want to choose peace or fear? Each is available to us at all times. If you find yourself in a room full of poo, look for the pony making it. What am I going to do today to make this a good, happy day?

Approach each day with excitement and wonder, looking for the evidence that the universe is lining things up for you. When you really put your intention out there and trust and believe, you will begin to see the signs of what you want manifesting. Yes, at times they may be just small signs. But by continually looking for the best in each situation, looking for the next rung on the ladder, no matter what else is going on around you, you will always see the leading light. What can I do to make this moment better? That is how you become successful in every endeavor. This is how you find your happiness and joyful life experience.

CHAPTER 6:
Appreciation: Ann's Story

I am living proof of all that I say. I speak from experience. One of my biggest miracles in my life happened after my mother transitioned in the beginning of 2011.

There was a time I was an owner of a real estate company in Florida and a large investor in oceanfront property in Fort Lauderdale. At this time I was a millionaire living the high life. I was jetting around the world and had multiple cars and homes. Then the real estate crash happened, and most everything I owned was worth less than the mortgages on them. The business began to fail, as did the economy. We struggled to keep everything going for a period of time, thinking things would get better, but they didn't. The expenses just kept outweighing any income. There was no option, and I was forced to close and file bankruptcy.

I wasn't sure of what was next, so I went back to my home

in New Jersey to try to get back to selling property there. As a Realtor you do not have a steady income; sometimes you need to work for months before you can close on a property and earn a commission. I found myself needing some immediate cash flow and health insurance. When I closed the company in Florida, I lost my insurance as well. I wondered what I could do.

One day while having a coffee in my neighborhood Starbucks, I learned that for only twenty hours a week, they provided their workers with very good health insurance. Many years previous I had owned a successful bagel and coffee shop, so I knew I really enjoyed this type of business. This seemed to be a perfect match for the moment.

Some of my contemporaries at the time thought I was silly for taking that type of job, thinking that it was beneath me. But there are times in life when you just need to do what you have to do. You cannot buy into others' opinions; just trust your instinct and do what feels right in the moment. So I decided to begin working at Starbucks. I accepted it as a task I had to do and allowed for the experience. Resistance was not an option.

Getting up early and serving coffee every morning may not have been what I really wanted to be doing at this point in my life, but I knew down deep that it would only be temporary and I might as well have fun and enjoy it. Yes, there were difficult moments, especially coming from driving a Mercedes and living on the beach just months before, but I was conscious of making each day fun and enjoyable. I found simple pleasure in making people smile with a joke or making friends with my coworkers. I liked to share stories, laugh, and keep a fun working atmosphere. Teamwork, cooperation, and fun were always the cornerstones of my previous businesses.

The store was only a ten-minute walk from my home, which was very convenient. I was able to find many blessings at this time—free coffee, for example! There were also many leftover sandwiches, cakes, and cookies when we closed, which I began bringing over to the local homeless shelters in the area. This brought me great joy. I did not allow myself to get depressed in this situation. I was not going to let my current circumstances dictate how I felt about myself. I would go to work and think to myself, *How can I make this a good day? How can I keep things fun?* I enjoyed brightening customers' days with a greeting of "Happy Monday" or "Happy Tuesday," depending on the day. What was important to me was to connect with the people around me and live for the day, enjoying the moments as best as possible. There were some tasks I did not really enjoy, such as cleaning the restrooms, but I accepted them and allowed the experience. I thought of it as a break from the customers or being on the line. I would change my perception about the task at hand and do what was in front of me without complaining.

I found my happiness in the anticipation of the good things to come in life, not reacting to the current situation.

Time went by, and miracles did manifest. I even became friendly with some Starbucks customers who became my real estate customers and bought their house through me. This I am sure was because of my happy, positive attitude.

I climbed up a little bit on the Starbucks ladder, first as a barista and then as a shift manager. Eventually I became a full-time assistant store manager. I chose to do this because I was trying to work out a loan modification on my primary residence in New Jersey. The bank said I needed a certain income to qualify, and taking a full-time management job was the quickest way to reach that income level.

I kept making the best choice in each moment to maintain a positive attitude and stay happy. Life was happening. I was having fun with my friends and doing a little traveling again, and then everything changed. The bank was not approving my modification and was becoming difficult to work with. Starbucks moved me to another location for their needs, and this was not comfortable for me anymore. There were challenges, and I felt that where I was no longer where I needed to be. However, I still trusted and participated in each day while looking positively toward the future.

Circumstances occurred, and I was presented with the opportunity to teach and travel in France for two months. I was so excited with the chance, and it felt right, so I jumped on it. I left Starbucks and flew to France. My experience there was wonderful on many levels. I was able to be with and teach exchange students I had hosted in the United States in the past. For many years I had been a host parent and New York City tour guide with LEC, a French student exchange program. During this trip to France I was able to visit the cities and the schools that the students had come from. I really enjoyed teaching with the teachers that I met during those years, who accompanied the groups when they came to the United States. My energy was definitely up and joyful as I traveled the country and was very warmly welcomed into the homes of new friends and old students.

I hated to eventually leave, but it came time to go home—and just in the nick of time! In early December I returned to my home in New Jersey and received the news that my mother, Ann, was sick. She lived in Orlando, Florida. All we knew at this point was that there was a mass in her stomach and it was probably cancer. This came as a surprise because otherwise she was in good health and went to the gym regularly. Just after Thanksgiving she noticed she was having stomach pain. She was dealing with it, just thinking it was indigestion, but it did not subside and was quickly getting worse. My aunt, her sister, finally got her to go to the doctor to check it out. It was then that they discovered the tumor, but they had no idea of the size or how it had already spread throughout all the abdominal organs. Luckily I had no immediate commitments and was able to go directly down to Florida to be with her.

I arrived in mid-December, just a week or so after the initial diagnosis. We were waiting for further oncology appointments. When I saw my mother, I could feel the gravity of the situation, but I was very happy to be there with her. It was important to me to keep her spirits up and make her as comfortable as possible. I was impressed with her calm manner in the situation. Every other small nuisance in life she had always made a huge deal about, but this time she was strangely accepting.

My thought was to take her on a cruise or someplace nice to relax, but she really did not feel like traveling and just wanted to stay home. Finally, after an appointment with the specialist, we were told the cancer was already stage four and inoperable, and she was given a life expectancy of three to six months. At the time we had no idea, but this was a gross overestimation. Christmas was the next week, and we focused on making the holiday an enjoyable time with the family. The day was perfect, a good combination of gifts, food, and family fun. Ann was really looking forward to a turkey dinner, which made us happy because she had had very little appetite.

The three days following Christmas were peaceful but uneventful. We were waiting to get an appointment with another oncologist to explore experimental options, but another problem was quickly developing. Her abdomen was distended, and her legs were becoming extremely swollen. I was very concerned and realized that we needed to get to a doctor right away. I brought her to a doctor, and we found out that she was developing blood clots in her legs because the liver was ceasing to function and fluid was building up in her lower body. She was admitted to the local hospital immediately and put into intensive care. Ann was a trooper. Through all of this she really remained calm and composed. I was very amazed. Thankfully some friends and family were able to come down right away to visit her in the hospital. We still had no idea that she had less than a week to live.

The hospital staff was really great and caring. The doctors ran many tests, and the results confirmed the gravity of the situation, which I somehow already knew inside. The time frame was reduced from months to weeks. Quickly we needed to have some serious discussions and make some decisions. Again, through all of this, Ann was coherent, composed, and in peace about what was transpiring. I felt it a true blessing to be with her through this.

New Year's had just passed, and there was nothing left the hospital could really do. Ann just wanted to go home. We decided home hospice was the best decision, because she definitely did not want to die in the hospital. Miraculously we were able to pull everything together quickly to make this happen. A hospital bed and other medical equipment were delivered to her home, and a comfortable place was created for Ann almost instantly after she made the decision. I still remember riding home with her in the ambulance; she was so happy and peaceful to be going home. She even joked about what to do with her stash of cartons of cigarettes and jars of coffee she had stored in the pantry.

We arrived home and got Ann settled into the hospital bed in her bedroom, complete with oxygen and all the supplies we could need. She was content. She even spoke on the phone with her friend back in Massachusetts whom she had sung with for many years. I was very happy to see her home and comfortable.

Ann's one and only evening back home was to be her last night in her body. Thankfully we had a nurse with us the whole time. I stayed up for a while making sure everything was going well and that the nurse had anything she needed. I finally got some sleep. Another nurse came in the morning to relieve the night nurse. I was impressed with how compassionately she was caring for my mother. The whole experience was amazingly beautiful and peaceful. For the most part Ann was sleeping and out of it at this point. It was about 9:30 in the morning when the nurse told me Ann was beginning to transition. I was shocked; I had no idea that she would pass so quickly. I guess she was content and happy to be home and ready to go. I called my aunt, her sister, and she and her husband came right over. The experience of Ann's passing was very peaceful and beautiful.

We were by her bed singing spiritual hymns and holding her hands. My mother's breathing slowed, she took a few last few breaths, and then she took one long exhale. Her spirit was free from the body. We all felt a definite sadness about her leaving and not having her physical presence around, but we were joyful because we knew that her spirit would be eternal.

My mother's passing was one of the most beautiful experiences I have ever had. To be with someone entering this world or leaving it is very powerful. It changed my whole attitude about death. There is definitely nothing to fear about it.

The service was lovely. Many friends and relatives came. One of her best friends, Gloria, even came with a few members of the Sweet Adeline chorus and sang. I showed the video of her skydiving out of an airplane with me. That was awesome!

CHAPTER 7:
Miracle

Retrain your thought process in how you look at things. This talent will assist you in every aspect of life. I always begin my day in appreciation of what is. I look forward with anticipation to the good experiences and the joy that will come my way. I often meditate briefly to center myself and become open to the possibilities the universe will present. I know I have the choice of where I want to focus my attention. I can discern what to think about to raise my energy and vibration.

One of my other passions many years ago was skydiving. I found a great sense of exhilaration and freedom in the sport. I was quickly hooked and began training with a 4-way formation skydiving team. I was part of three different teams while I was in the sport. We would practice mainly in southern New Jersey at Cross Keys Drop Zone, or at The Ranch in

Gardner, New York. On occasion we would go to the wind tunnel in Orlando, ironically next to where I practice Trapeze and Aerial Silks currently. Often we would travel to Drop Zones in other states for meets and competitions. No, it wasn't who could fall the fastest. We competed against other teams by creating different formations while we were falling, which were video taped, and then viewed on the ground by judges who counted the number of grips, or formations, that we completed in a specified amount of time. It was great! I really enjoyed the friends I made and being part of a team. During my last competition I had an accident and crushed my leg. I was devastated.

This began a very challenging period for me. After a serious operation where they took my knee apart and inserted a titanium rod up to my hip, I had a very long recuperation. I was in bed for weeks with my leg in a machine that kept bending and flexing the knee joint. Obviously, I could not work, which meant I had little money coming in because I was self-employed. I did work hard at my leg therapy and pushed myself as much as I could, but I definitely had some down days. A close friend had introduced my to Bijan Anjomi and his wife Samia who ran Effortless Prosperity seminars. This opened the door to a tremendous transformational period for me. By taking ego and judgment out of the equation I began to see experiences for what they really are, opportunities for healing and growth. They were both caring, inspiring and assisted me to reconnect to my source.

I had attended many of their Effortless Prosperity seminars in various cities around America and in Cancun, Mexico. My sense of self and my connection to the universal source grew immensely. I could truly begin to see that all things work together for my greatest good when I allow, and have my main goal be peace and joy. I was originally scheduled to attend one of these seminars being held in Playa del Carmen the same month my mother transitioned.

Because she was ill and given a three-month window, I had to cancel my attendance. She passed on the sixth of January, and the service was on the thirteenth. By this time half of the seminar was over, but I felt a strong inspiration inside that guided me to fly as quickly as I could to Mexico and attend the last half. Only a few of my close friends attending the seminar knew what had just happened, but I was there and very sure that was where I should be. My mother always supported me living life to the fullest, and I was certain she approved. I felt deep joy and appreciation in what I had just experienced, along with a feeling of being complete, having been with her through to the end. Some people thought I should be in mourning, but I knew her energy was more with me now than ever before.

I met many new people at this seminar; there were a large

number of attendees from China. Bijan had expanded his seminars to Asia in the previous year, which brought many new faces to the annual Cancun seminar. I was very familiar with everyone from the United States and Canada, as I had been an avid participant for many years. I had learned very much and become so much more spiritually open than I had ever been in my life, listening to and following his teachings. As always, I was present in the moment and open to whatever blessings might come.

In everything I did at that seminar, I knew my joy and connection shined through, because an amazing Chinese woman was attracted to my energy. She enjoyed my sharing and my singing and felt drawn to my energy. By the end of the seminar she asked me if I would be interested in going to China to speak and share my thoughts. Initially I was surprised and wondered if she was serious. But the wheels were in motion and the energy was flowing. In just a month's time I found myself flying first class to China to begin a whole new chapter in my life.

Since that flight four years ago, I have been traveling all over China as a motivational speaker, giving seminars, doing personal coaching, and spreading my joy. I have been so very blessed in China. Everywhere I go I am welcomed warmly. Each day I look for the joy in whatever I am doing. There is so much opportunity everywhere I go. I don't really have much downtime because on my free days I teach English to junior high school students.

As I shared before, all my life I have been involved in personal growth and development, along with all of my own business endeavors. I have spoken and shared my story in many seminars over the years. I talk about how I was featured as the person who lives life to the fullest in the movie *The Answer*. I was filmed in my oceanfront home at the time, talking about my business and my history, but best of all showing how I enjoy life by flying an L-39 fighter jet, jet skiing in my backyard, and tooling around Fort Lauderdale in my convertible. At this time I thought I had hit a high. But no, I had to lose almost everything to get where I am now and to be able to share my story and inspire others. My life is an amazing journey, which is how I can share my story and show you how all of this really works when you are open and allowing. When you trust the flow to carry you, it will always bring you effortlessly to where you want to go for your highest good. When you make how you feel more important than what is going on around you and listen to your inner guidance system, you will create miracles.

CHAPTER 8:
Inspired Action

The law of attraction requires action! Many fans of the law of attraction think you don't need to take any action. You simply sit like a magnet and wait for your good vibes to slide the thing you want over to you. I believe that you usually, if not always, have to take action of some sort. However, your action does not have to be effort if it comes from your heart. Do it because you want to do it, because it bubbles out of your passion to do it, and then it's not effort. This is inspired action. Again, the law of attraction doesn't mean you don't do anything; it means what you do is without effort. It is all in how you set up and perceive your goal. To me, the law of attraction works to make life easier, but not because you don't take action, because the action you take is natural for you. Thought plus action equals results. From their vision and inspiration, many people have made huge successes; they have had a drive and boldness to act. When you come from your passion, using the tools and blessings we each have, you can create miracles. A miracle that touches or benefits just one person is still a miracle. We all have the power to make a difference.

All my life I have been oriented by action. My strong sense of self, which I thank my mother for, inspired me to do many exciting things in my life. I became a working actor and model in New York City, doing commercials, plays, soap operas, and magazine advertisements. I owned and operated Bagel Dish, a bagel bakery and coffee store in Highland Park, New Jersey, for almost fifteen years, and I was featured in *Entrepreneur* magazine in 1993. I had an antique shop in New Hope, Pennsylvania, and another one in Hopewell, New Jersey, years later. I created an American restaurant named Dish Café in New Jersey. I owned Barricini Hallmark, a card and gift shop in New Brunswick, New Jersey—one of my favorite jobs, because it was a clean, non-food business, and I had a wonderful retired women working for me. I was a broker manager of preferred properties in Highland Park, New Jersey, as well as a broker owner of a Keller Williams realty office in Fort Lauderdale, Florida. Over the years I owned and managed many rental properties, some of which I had renovated and flipped back when you could. I had a horse years ago and liked riding English and jumping. After that I learned figure skating and even won a medal.

Once I turned thirty, my tastes became more thrilling. I fell in love with skydiving and became a licensed pilot. I embraced the sense of freedom and possibility being aloft gave me. Through the years I was a member of three skydiving teams and competed in four-way formation skydiving. I also body flew in a few large multiway jumps until my accident at a competition, which I explained earlier. Traveling is another huge passion of mine; I have visited many countries around the world and explored many historic sites.

I have always thought of myself as a big kid. I retain my youthful exuberance. I think this has helped me enormously in creating and experiencing all the things I have done in my life. Have you ever noticed the passion and excitement children exhibit? We were all born with this wonderful curiosity and eagerness, but it seems to disappear as we grow older. This is what we should rediscover in order to believe again what life is truly about: the joyful experience.

A child looks at an experience with eagerness and without expectation. As adults we attach so much to the outcome or bring overwhelming fear to the process so that we lose sight of what is right in front of us. In this moment of the reality that we currently face, whether it's an obstacle or an exciting experience, the most useful tool we have is our awareness.

The present is the most important moment. This is the dime upon which our whole life could change, depending on the decision we make and the inspired action we take. There are some people who unknowingly choose play a victim and say they had no choice. They stumble through each situation and then complain about the outcome later. This behavior does not serve your best interest. We all have the power to influence our destiny. We must become aware that each of us is an amazing creator. We are always creating, every single day. However, many people create unconsciously and have things show up in their lives that they do not really want to manifest. When we learn to create consciously and focus our thoughts, the things that we want will show up in our life. Once we get connected to our inner power, our source, we are then open to the inspiration and are guided to choose what will bring us joy and happiness. Be childlike and open to inspiration in the moment. Do not complicate or overthink things. Life should be simple. Participate in the moment. Feel for the inspired action inside as it bubbles up from within.

Create your future one day at a time. To have a different result tomorrow, you must make different choices today. Each new moment is a chance to make a positive choice. Choose peace and joy to create a brighter future. That is the best way to have a joyful life. Embrace each new day as an opportunity, not an obstacle. Access the guidance of source and spirit, and you will be led in the direction that will bring you peace and joy. Doors will open, and opportunities will present themselves that are in alignment with your inner desires.

You will still have to take action and work on what life presents, but it will be effortless and enjoyable. You will want to participate fully, and the experiences will actually be fun and even exciting. Change your perceptions, and you will change your life. Through the years we have attached so much fear and untrue meaning to things. When we break through these old beliefs and truly release them, we are then open to experiencing a joyous lifestyle.

I am still amazed each day as my wants and desires manifest so easily. I just focus on what I want to create or achieve, put it out to the universe with loving and joyful energy, and then watch how the events unfold. All this takes is practice. Like an athlete trains his body, mind, and skills, we too have to train ourselves in what we say, think, and do. Live life to the fullest. Consciously and joyfully create!

CHAPTER 9:
Shenyang Seminar: Living Joyfully!

Happy Wednesday! I love living joyfully! The way that I live my life is what I would like to bring to you, to help you to create and enjoy some of the same miracles that I find in my life every day. I want to tell you about my joyful life seminar, which is what I created in China, in which I share the ways that I have been able to create miracles and joy in my life. Every day is wonderful. Every day there is incredible opportunity out there. Reach for the best thought and action each day, and you will reach your goal. The problem is many of us get burdened down with the day-to-day issues and with what life sometimes seems to thrust at us. There are many responsibilities that we have. We have many things to care for, such as our families, our work, and our friends. Sometimes these can be very overwhelming and we don't know how to balance everything in our life.

You may find yourself being successful in one way, such as in business, but then have a difficult family life that you suffer from. Maybe you have a wonderful family but you're having difficulty in business and your work isn't going well, which causes a lot of emotional and economic stress. On the other hand, financially you can be in evergreen, but you have marital problems and trouble with your children. Whatever this issue is, you find yourself frustrated and unhappy. These are some of the common situations that I find with the clients I have had the opportunity to coach. And I'm here to tell you that you can have everything.

What does a joyful life mean? A joyful life is a life filled with happiness and joy. You have excellent health, wonderful relationships, abundance of wealth, and a peaceful life.

Think of this as an umbrella under which your life is comfortable and secure. I know you're thinking that's impossible and you can't have it all. But you can have it all! My goal is to show you how to do it and give you techniques that you can use to create the life you have always wanted. This begins by opening your mind to the universal principles and laws that exist all around us. These simple truths govern the energy that connects all things.

First of all, and most important, fear exists only in the mind. It is the excuse we give ourselves so we don't have to try. Limiting beliefs are just that: beliefs that have no truth to them other than what is in your own mind. In life I have found that there are three types of people: runners, spectators, and those who commit to what they're doing. Runners are the type of people who always run from the things that need to be done; spectators are the ones who stand around and watch everybody else do the work; and then there are the people who just belt up and get the job done.

I believe in the Nike slogan, "Just do it." Everything else is just excuses. What type of person are you? How long have you been that way? Does it serve you well in life? Make your decision, ask for what you want, and put it out into the universe. Feel good about where you are, but look forward with anticipation to having your desires manifest. Let go of any attachment to the outcome; always find your happiness in each moment. It is more important to find the emotion first and embody the joyful feeling about what you want before it can manifest.

You always create what you are thinking about. Wherever you focus your attention, you will see the physical creation that comes from that. You do manifest the good and the bad, the wanted and the unwanted. If you are trying to solve a dilemma and you keep talking about the problem, then that is what you are going to create more of—problems. Release your grip on what was, and shift your focus to what you want and how you will feel when you get it. Positive vibration brings positive results while negative vibration brings negative results.

Come from the place of being the blank slate or page upon which the universe will fill everything else in. In order to have anything in your life, there needs to be an open space into which it can come. It is drawn to you with the knowing that you are worthy and deserving of all that you desire. Creation flows when you are open to the possibility of letting the universe give you the blessings that are yours already.

Many of us have forgotten who we are—we are all powerful and amazing creators. I want to remind you that every day we are creating, and the important thing is to be creating consciously, not unconsciously. Become aware of the things you're focusing your attention on. Your thoughts are like a big magnet pulling things toward you. Don't play the victim of your own creation. Become a victorious, conscious creator; it just takes a little effort and practice. When you take responsibility for everything you've created in your life, you then become empowered to change whatever does not bring you joy.

Your true power lies inside, not outside. Again I want to remind you of your incredible power and the inheritance that is yours to accept. Raise your awareness daily. Be present in each moment and practice "right here, right now." I am living proof that when you are open and willing to be a cooperative component with the universe and everything around you, the miracles and blessings do come. The cornerstone of my joy is knowing that in each moment I am content and complete because I am certain all is perfect. There is always perfection in *now*, and when you realize that it is always now, you can be open to finding the peace that is always available. You can find all your power in the "right here, right now."

Everybody lives the same three days over and over again: yesterday, today, and tomorrow. I challenge you to think about what day you live mostly in. The people living in yesterday just focus on the anger, resentment, and guilt from events in their past. Some carry the sadness from situations they wished they had handled differently. The people who live in tomorrow live mostly for the future. They say, "Well, I'm doing this now because in so many years I'll be happy" or "I will be happy when this happens or that happens." The end will justify the means. Others let the fear of what may or may not happen tomorrow limit their happiness today. They are too afraid to make a different choice, so they just keep repeating the same thing day after day.

People who live in today are the most powerful. They are open, ready, aware, and able to handle whatever life brings to them each day. All your power is in today. Whatever happened in the past is gone. It's done; it's finished. Just let it go. As the Bible says in Matthew chapter 8 "the dead will bury their own dead". There is nothing that you can do to change the events in the past; all you can do is accept them, learn from them, and move on.

As for fear, it doesn't really exist; it is something we all create in our minds, and it is not real. Fear is just the excuse we give to remain mediocre. It is time to look at the limiting beliefs in our life, the things that are holding us back from having a fulfilling, happy, and joyful life, and release them. Why are many people waiting to live? So many people think they are working to better their tomorrow, but tomorrow never comes. It's like running after the horizon: as you keep running toward it, you see it move farther away. You never reach it; you keep running and tiring yourself out until you die. That is life for many people. What kind of life do you consciously want to choose?

Live for today and embrace the deliciousness that each new moment brings. Be open to the possibilities that life holds for us when we allow our dreams to shape our futures. Enjoy the journey, appreciate where you are, and look forward to the wonderful possibilities that you are now assured you will create. Life's true excitement resides in each new day. All you need to do to feel this is watch a sunrise; feel the loving, warm energy radiate to you. Reach for the best feeling and thought you can each day that will allow you to be a matching vibration to your desires.

You can change your life in an instant when you change your perception about the events today. It is all up to you. Life is simple. You possess all the power you need to change the direction of your life. My life is excellent because I've learned to let go of the things in the past, dispel the fear of tomorrow, and find my joy each day. Right here, right now, I am in control of my life. I am constantly creating what I want to show up in my experience by flowing with the universal energy and being a cooperative component. I am in control of where I want my life to go. I am the only captain of my ship. I will focus on the present and all the good things going on in my life. I know that I can create consistent abundance in my life.

We all deserve a joyful life—a happy family, success in work, wonderful relationships, and plenty of time to enjoy this amazing planet we live on. Everything I focus on in my mind will show up, so I know that I am capable of success with all of this. When you are tuned in to your source, everything begins to flow effortlessly. It is the law of the universe. It is the law of attraction. You manifest into your life whatever is in your consciousness.

Use the technique "right here, right now" to observe what is good in your life. If you can't see something directly in your immediate experience, then go more general. Look broader at your moment until you can see the good and find something to appreciate. It is more important to fix your mind and emotion on happiness and joy than to push against a problem and create more resistance. By shifting your perception, you create an opening for the energy to enter your experience and guide you through it and inspire your action. Look for what is working. What can you do to make things better? By asking yourself questions, you may begin to see possibilities and open up a new perspective. All the true power is deep inside and available to us at any moment just by opening up and allowing.

Most people focus with the mass consciousness and its belief systems. They give up their power and look elsewhere for direction because they have forgotten how to use the guidance system we were born with. Our emotions are really indicators of our alignment with our higher selves. When we experience negative emotions like frustration, sadness, anger, and resentment, it is only a wakeup call to let us know that we need to shift our perception about the situation because we are out of alignment with who we really are. The faster we are aware of this, we begin to shift and will see our lives opening up and becoming effortless. You will begin to see things for what they really are and not attach so many old beliefs, which only serve to bring up negative emotion.

When we are open to making good choices, when we are open to allowing the best choice for our life in the moment, the miracles will begin to flow in. Let the energy of the flow carry you, and then watch for the inspired action and follow it. The work will then seem fun. You will enjoy the effort you put into your work and derive greater satisfaction from it. You never know what will manifest and from where when you are open and allowing. There will be so many more possibilities that will present themselves.

By living my life with my foundation principles and following the laws of the universe, I know I am secure. No matter what happens in my life, as long as I am present in the moment, I know that what is best for my life will come to me. I'm here to show you through my life and experience that there is an effortless way to have everything that you want in your life. Even the things you thought you wanted may shift. Life is always evolving, and our desires are ever changing based on the new circumstance that we create. You will find a renewed excitement as you begin to see the evidence in your life manifest. Life is joyful when we live as we are created to live.

When we were born, we came into the world open, innocent, and excited. But what happens? As we begin to grow up and are affected by our environment, we create many limiting belief systems. We learn fear. If you do this, that will happen. The truth is fear does not exist. It is learned and created in the mind. We use it as an excuse or a crutch. The people we learn these things from are well meaning, but the result is that we begin to live in scarcity and fear. We believe these things about ourselves, and it affects the way we live and experience life. Listen to yourself. Most people are taught to be more interested in what others think they should do and feel, and they have lost calibration with their own guidance. Look inside and notice what makes you feel good. Pay intention to the inspiration inside.

We are all, each of us, limitless, wonderful spiritual beings. We all have a vibration, as does everything around us. We should be more concerned about our vibration and less concerned about outside events. It doesn't matter what happens in life. What matters is how we feel about it. When we make this our primary goal, anything is possible.

My own life is a testament to that. The people who have known me for years have seen that I am always happy, just like a big kid. Many people have said, "How can you always be happy? It is not possible." My response is that I am not happy all the time; I am only happy today. I find my happiness in each moment. I know that in each moment, regardless of the situation, I am going to reach for the best possible thought and feeling I can. I understand that right here, right now; I will find the love in what I am doing. By being happy for this moment, and it's always this moment, the result gives me a joyful life—happy today, happy the next day, and happy the day after that. The days become weeks, the weeks become months, the months become years, and the years equal a happy life!

Be most concerned with how you are feeling in the now; tomorrow will take care of itself. If you just focus on today, this moment, you seize your power. It is good to have plans and goals, but be present in the moment and realize where you are focusing your attention. Am I doing the things that I need to do today that will achieve the goal I want to get to? Have an open mind, and be aware and open to the inspired action. I am most concerned with my relationship with my feelings and myself. Am I keeping the channels open and clear to hear the messages?

My goal is to remind you of your power—remind you of who you really are inside. We are all born worthy of creating a wonderful and joyous life. We all have the same amazing inheritance when can connect with our source. Life is meant to be good. We are here to expand our experiences and enjoy interacting with each other. We are here to live and enjoy the blessing of life. That is what life should be—that is what it can be! The only thing standing in our way is our own limitations and ourselves. We hold ourselves back from achieving our dreams. If we could just stop doing those things, we would take giant leaps forward. We can have it all!

Shift your perception, and you can change your life. All it takes is one moment—this present moment—to make the decision to let go of the crap in my life. It can be gone in an instant. The past is the past. We all deserve a good life. We all deserve to be good to ourselves and to each other. Love yourself. Forgive yourself. Release your negative belief systems. Accept yourself just as you are, and then the possibilities are limitless. Create a loving relationship with yourself. Become clear on what you do want in your life, and focus daily on the good things. Discover the joy in life.

When I get up in the morning, I am excited. I become clear that my intention is to live the best day I possibly can. I trust. I know that everything is already taken care of, if I can only allow it to be. A joyful life requires the daily choice to care about yourself and how you feel in relation to what is going on around you. Always bring yourself into the present moment—right here, right now.

Pay attention to the inspiration inside. Break through your resistance, and be open to the pure positive energy that will flow through you when you allow it. Find your daily harmony that will give you the joy and the passionate inspiration to achieve all you want to create in this life. Life is as amazing and incredible as you will allow it to be. I wish for each of us a very joyful life.

This chapter is actual content taken from a seminar the author gave in Shenyang, China, in 2012.

CHAPTER 10:
Change Your Perception and Change Your Life!

We only have control over ourselves. If happiness depends on other people, so much energy is wasted on what there is no control over. You become frustrated and create negative emotions. It is so hard even to change the closest of friends or an immediate family member. But to find peace and happiness, you just have to change yourself and your perceptions. It is so much easier. If you do not depend on anyone, or on any situation, and focus on yourself, the whole world changes beautifully.

By being in the present moment and aware of my mind and my emotions, I am not concerned with what others think. I take control of my mind and what I am about to create. This technique of "right here, right now" is so beautiful. We only have to change ourselves because when we change our mind, our perception shifts and the world starts to look beautiful for each of us. It's what's going within our mind that affects the way we see things. This changes the way I see the world in front of me. If I feel good, automatically I notice positive things. If I feel bad, even the good things will start to look not so good and I will create worry.

Everything is about the change within. It's not about what is happening around me. It's more about the way I perceive it and feel about it. Change your mind and make your life beautiful and happy. This is why we are all living, for us to experience joy and be happy. Living in the moment is such a beautiful way for this to happen. Change your perception, and you can change your life!

Our mission is to awaken others and ourselves to the fact that we each have the power to create the life and experience we want. We have given away so much of our power to the beliefs we have learned from our family, our culture, and our religion. The truth is that we are and have always been connected to our source. We are an extension of that source, and we possess power and ability beyond our current understanding. By releasing our limiting belief systems and reclaiming our own power, we can take control of our life and what we experience. By being aware moment to moment and seeing the truth, we are open to inspiration and can then act on it. Rather than unconsciously reacting, we each liberate ourselves from our perceived powerlessness and become the effective manifestors we came here to be.

Become aware of what you think about. It is very important to control your point of focus. How you feel inside determines how you view the outside. What you focus on, on the outside, is what you bring into your life experience. So when you are in a bad mood or depressed, that is all that you see around you, and therefore you create more of the same experience. But when you come from joy and shift your perspective on the events you experience, a whole new world opens up for you. You realize you can be in the world but not of it. You will attract more positive experiences into your life.

This moment is the mother of each coming moment. Each new moment we have the opportunity to give birth to new creation, a new moment. By being in the present and not influenced by negative past experiences, we can make clear choices and be open to inspiration.

The clearest truth is in the present moment. The past is gone, and the future is uncertain. All your power comes from the *now*, observing it as it is, without judgment and past beliefs. Only when we realize this are we able to take action with our conscious mind and not react with our unconscious mind. That is how we can manifest the positive things in our life and create the experiences we were born to have.

The past is history, the future is a mystery, and today is a gift. That is why it is called the present. As with any gift, it is up to you what you choose to do with it.

I wish each of you a joyful, happy, fulfilling life!

For more information please visit:

www.EricDonlan.com